Dr. Shirley R. **BROWN**, Th.D

PRIDE
ANGER
REJECTION
UNFORGIVENESS
MALICE
FEAR

WALKING WITH THE DEMONS OF YOUR PAST

Exposing the Past, Dismantling Strongholds, and Walking in Freedom

WALKING WITH THE DEMONS OF YOUR PAST

Exposing the Past, Dismantling Strongholds, and Walking in Freedom

Dr. Shirley R. **BROWN**, Th.D

CONCISE
PUBLISHING HOUSE

Walking with the Demons of Your Past: Exposing the Past, Dismantling Strongholds, and Walking in Freedom

©2025 by Dr. Shirley R. Brown, Th.D All rights reserved.

ISBN: 979-8-9909626-5-1

No part of this publication may be reproduced, distributed, or transmitted in any form or by any means, including photocopying, recording, or other electronic or mechanical methods, without the prior written permission of the publisher, except in the case of brief quotations embodied in critical reviews and certain other noncommercial uses permitted by copyright law. For permission requests, write to the publisher, addressed

"Attention: Permissions Coordinator," at the address below.

Concise Publishing House
120 Preston Executive Drive Suite 229
Cary, NC 27513

www.ConcisePublishing.us

Scriptures marked NKJV are taken from the NEW KING JAMES VERSION (NKJV): © 1982 by Thomas Nelson, Inc. Used by permission. All rights reserved. Scriptures marked NLT are taken from the NEW LIVING TRANSLATION (NLT): © 1996, 2004, 2007 by Tyndale House Foundation. Used by permission of Tyndale House Publishers. All rights reserved. Used by permission. Scripture quotations marked MSG are taken from THE MESSAGE, ©1993, 2002, 2018 by Eugene H. Peterson. Used by permission of NavPress, represented by Tyndale House Publishers. All rights reserved. Scriptures marked ESV are taken from the ENGLISH STANDARD VERSION: Copyright © 2016 by Crossway. Used by permission. All rights reserved.

Dedication

To every son and daughter who has mistaken a wound for an identity—may the Healer rename you.

Acknowledgements

First and foremost, I give honor and glory to God, the true author and finisher of my life. Without His guidance, wisdom, and sustaining grace, this work could not exist. Every chapter is a testament to His faithfulness and His desire to heal and transform me first so others could see HIM.

To my family – thank you for your unwavering love, encouragement, and patience. Your prayers, support, and belief in this calling and the seasons of growth, healing, and deliverance.

To my spiritual leaders, mentors, thank you for pouring into me, challenging me, and helping shape the voice of God in me.

To my church community and those who walked with me in ministry, I deeply appreciate your support and your hunger.

To everyone that supported in any way thank you for going on this journey. To those that have struggles, and questions ..let's do it , seek God and pursue transformation.

From my heart a simple Thank You.

Contents

INTRODUCTION 1
The Silent Companions

CHAPTER 1 5
The Shadows That Speak

CHAPTER 2 11
When Pain Becomes Identity

CHAPTER 3 17
The Familiar Spirit of the Old Self

CHAPTER 4 23
Forgiveness — The Gate of Release

CHAPTER 5 29
The Power of Confrontation

CHAPTER 6 35
Healing the Fractured Soul

CHAPTER 7 43
Breaking the "Recycle"

CHAPTER 8 51
Walking in Newness

CHAPTER 9 59
The Journey Continues

Appendix 65

6 Steps to Self-Deliverance 65

INTRODUCTION
The Silent Companions

There are pains we learned to walk with long before we ever learned to name them. Wounds that never quite healed. Memories that never fully faded. Traumas we tucked into the corners of our souls, hoping time would bury them—only to discover that time does not heal what we refuse to confront. These unaddressed places, these silent companions, travel with us through the years. They sit in the shadows of our decisions. They whisper in moments of vulnerability. They rise whenever life presses us in familiar ways.

Many never realize that unresolved pain can become its own presence—almost alive, almost breathing—shaping behavior, bending choices, and quietly sabotaging relationships. The past, when never brought to the Cross, does not stay behind us. It grows into a force that influences the present. It becomes the uninvited counselor interpreting our world through broken lenses. It becomes the familiar voice that tells us who we are, who we are not, and what we can never become.

These are the demons of the past—not creatures with horns, but internal strongholds built through memory, emotion, and spiritual imprint. They are the remnants of battles we survived but never overcame. The residue of seasons that ended, yet still live in us as if they never did. They feed on the moments we replay, the wounds we protect, and the truths we avoid. They show up as fear, insecurity, anger, shame, perfectionism, abandonment, guilt, and the cycles we promised ourselves we would never repeat again.

This book was written to expose those hidden forces. To shine a prophetic light on the shadows that have grown too comfortable. To help you discern the roots of the cycles you keep reliving. And to guide you through the courageous journey of confronting what has walked with you long enough.

At the end of each chapter, you will find a section titled *Notes for Freedom Walking* — a sacred space for reflection, honesty, and partnering with the Holy Spirit as He continues your healing.

My assignment here is not merely to inform you—it is to lead you toward deliverance. A deliverance that not only frees you from the grip of the past but restores what the past tried to steal. A deliverance that untangles your identity, reclaims your voice, heals your inner world, and positions you for the destiny you were always predestined to live.

You do not have to walk with the silent companions any longer. You do not have to bow to the demons of the past.

There is a way to move forward. There is a way out.

And there is a way into the life your soul has been crying for.

This journey begins here.

CHAPTER 1
The Shadows That Speak

"And He asked him, 'What is your name?' And he answered, saying, 'My name is Legion; for we are many.'" **Mark 5:9 ESV**

There are moments in life when your past does not whisper — it screams. It echoes through your emotions, your reactions, your decisions. Though you are born again, Spirit-filled, and walking in purpose, something from yesterday keeps tugging at the hem of your deliverance. These are the shadows that speak — the unresolved, unhealed, and unrenounced fragments of who you were before Christ's full dominion took hold.

We call them demons of the past not because they always manifest in dramatic forms, but because they are the unseen companions of pain. They hide in memories, reactions, and silent agreements. They disguise themselves as personality traits, defense mechanisms, or "just how I am." Yet beneath the surface lies something spiritual — something that must be confronted, named, and cast out by truth.

When Jesus met the man among the tombs, He didn't just see a tormented body — He saw a tormented history. The question "What is your name?" was not for information; it was for revelation. Christ was demanding the past to identify itself. In that same way, before true healing can come, you must confront the names of your own pain.

The Language of the Past

Every wound speaks a language. Betrayal says, "Never trust again. "Abandonment whispers, "You are not worth staying for." Rejection screams, "You are unlovable. "These phrases become the internal vocabulary of bondage.

But the Lord, in His mercy, come s to translate the language of pain into the language of purpose. *Isaiah 61 ESV* reminds us that He came *"to bind up the brokenhearted, to proclaim liberty to the captives, and the opening of the prison to them that are bound."* The anointing does not simply silence your past; it reveals and redefines it. What once was your tomb becomes your testimony.

Emotional Residue and Spiritual Strongholds

You can be saved but still shackled.

You can speak in tongues but still be tied to trauma.

Deliverance is not just the casting out of spirits — it is the eviction of emotional residue that gives those spirits room to return.

When Paul wrote, *"Be transformed by the renewing of your mind" (Romans 12:2 KJV),* He was not speaking of mere positive thinking. He was describing a spiritual renovation — the process of removing what was built by pain and rebuilding according to the pattern of truth. Some believers pray for deliverance but refuse to surrender their thought patterns. Yet the greatest battlefield is not the altar — it is the mind.

Cycles and the Familiar

The demons of the past love cycles — repeated patterns of failure that keep you circling the same mountain. *Deuteronomy 2:3 AMP* says, *"You have circled this mountain long enough; turn northward."*

Cycles are proof that something familiar has taken residence. Familiar spirits are not always generational; sometimes they are emotional patterns passed down through learned behavior. You saw how your mother withdrew when she was hurt, so now withdrawal feels natural. You watched your father shut down in anger, so now silence becomes your form of control. The spirit of the familiar convinces you that dysfunction is comfort. But God calls you to confront what has become normal — because what feels normal is often what keeps you bound.

The Confrontation of the Cross

Deliverance is confrontation — not with demons first, but with truth. The Cross is not only a place of forgiveness; it is a mirror. It shows you what must die so that Christ might live through you.

Jesus never delivered anyone He did not first confront. In *Mark 5*, He confronted Legion. *In John 5:6 KJV*, He confronted the man at the pool, asking, *"Do you want to be made whole?"* Wholeness requires agreement — you must want to be free more than you want to be right.

Freedom is costly. It demands you lay down excuses and pick up exposure. But once you stand in the light, the shadows lose their power. The demons of your past cannot dwell where revelation shines.

Apostolic Insight

Deliverance without discipleship leads to relapse. Many are set free at the altar but never walk free in their daily life because they were delivered from a spirit but never discipled into truth. Apostolic deliverance restores both order and identity — it tears down what hell built and establishes what Heaven designed.

You cannot just walk out of your past; you must build new pathways of thought, worship, and obedience. Each act of surrender becomes a brick in your new foundation.

Beloved, this is where your journey begins — confronting the shadows, naming them, and declaring that their language no longer speaks for you.

Notes for Freedom Walking

The Shadows That Speak

CHAPTER 2
When Pain Becomes Identity

"And He said unto me, My grace is sufficient for thee: for my strength is made perfect in weakness." **2 Corinthians 12:9 KJV**

Pain was never meant to be a permanent garment, yet many have worn it so long it feels like skin. There comes a moment when pain stops being an event and becomes a definition — who you think you are. You no longer just remember the wound; you become it.

Some wear pain like a badge of honor — "I've survived so much." Others hide it under layers of performance, laughter, and ministry activity. But no matter the disguise, pain that is not healed becomes identity, and identity that is shaped by pain attracts bondage.

When you begin to introduce yourself by what broke you — "I'm divorced," "I was betrayed," "I was abandoned" — you unknowingly declare allegiance to your injury. The enemy uses this as a spiritual passport, granting him continued access to your emotional territory.

The Subtle Covenant of the Wounded

Every time you say, "I'll never let anyone hurt me again," you form a vow that binds rather than frees. Those inner covenants are spiritual contracts — agreements that build walls where God wants to place bridges. *Proverbs 18:21 KJV* reminds us, *"Death and life are in the power of the tongue."* Many have spoken death over their own freedom by making promises rooted in pain.

Deliverance begins when you renounce those silent vows. You must unbind yourself from the words that you meant for protection, but which became prisons.

The False Strength of Survival

Survival feels powerful. It says, "I made it." But survival without healing creates hardness — and hardness is not strength; it is scar tissue around the heart.

God never called you to merely survive; He called you to live. In *John 10:10 KJV*, Jesus declares, *"I am come that they might have life, and that they might have it more abundantly."* The abundant life cannot flow through walls of self-protection. You cannot drink from the well of abundance while guarding your heart with fear.

True strength is not in never breaking — it's

in letting the Lord rebuild you after the breaking.

Brokenness becomes holy when it becomes surrendered. That's why Paul could boast in weakness — because he understood that his cracks were conduits for grace.

When Pain Becomes Personality

Some believers confuse deliverance with denial. They say, "That's just how I am," but the Holy Spirit says, "No, that's how you became."

Pain can shape behavior so deeply that the person forgets who they were before the wound. Sarcasm, isolation, control, manipulation — these are not personality traits; they are trauma responses that have become identities.

God is not trying to change your personality — He's trying to restore your purity. Your temperament was divinely designed, but trauma distorted it. The Apostle Peter was passionate, but before Pentecost his passion lacked direction. Jesus didn't remove his fire — He purified it. Likewise, God will not extinguish your drive or your discernment; He will heal the motive behind it.

Healing the Memory, Not Erasing It

Healing does not erase the memory; it removes the sting. The Cross does not make you forget; it makes you free.

Joseph remembered what his brothers did, but by the time they bowed before him, he no longer bled from the memory. He could say, *"You meant evil against me, but God meant it for good" (Genesis 50:20 ESV).*

The proof of healing is not forgetfulness — it's freedom. When you can recall what happened without reliving the pain, you know deliverance has reached the soul.

Reclaiming the Mirror

James 1:23–25 ESV speaks of those who look in a mirror and immediately forget what manner of person they are. Pain distorts the mirror — it makes you see your reflection through the lens of what was done to you instead of who you were created to be.

But the Word of God restores the mirror. Each verse you declare, each truth you embrace, wipes away another smudge until you begin to see yourself again — healed, whole, and holy.

Apostolic Insight

Deliverance from pain is not emotional amnesia; it is emotional authority. When you rule over what once ruled you, you step into dominion. Apostolic grace teaches believers not just to weep at the altar but to walk in authority beyond it.

Pain must no longer define you. You are not what happened to you — you are what survived it, and more importantly, what was redeemed through it.

You are not the wound; you are the weapon God forged through it.

Notes for Freedom Walking

When Pain Becomes Identity

CHAPTER 3
The Familiar Spirit of the Old Self

"You have circled this mountain long enough; now turn northward." ***Deuteronomy 2:3 AMP***

There comes a time when you must recognize that what feels familiar is not always what is divine. The greatest danger to deliverance is not always the devil — it is the desire to return to what you've been freed from. Familiarity is seductive; it feels safe, predictable, even comforting. But it is also the very atmosphere where bondage breathes.

When Israel came out of Egypt, they were physically free but mentally bound. Every time pressure came, their hearts turned backward. They said, "It was better for us in Egypt." That's what the familiar spirit does — it paints bondage as comfort and freedom as risk. It makes you long for the past because the past doesn't demand transformation.

The Spirit of Familiarity

The familiar spirit does not always come through witchcraft; often, it manifests through memory. It's the unhealed part of you that wants what's easy instead of what's right. It whispers, "Go back to what you know." But deliverance will always require departure.

When God told Abram, *"Go from your country, your kindred, and your father's house" (Genesis 12:1 ESV),* He was not only calling him geographically forward — He was calling him emotionally away. Abram had to break covenant with what was known to receive what was promised.

You cannot carry Egypt into Canaan and expect to conquer. Every time God brings you into a new place, He demands a new posture. Familiar spirits keep you rehearsing what used to be instead of embracing what God is forming now.

Cycles and Patterns: The Language of the Familiar

Familiarity shows itself through cycles — the same arguments, the same temptations, the same emotional triggers, over and over again. These are not coincidences; they are spiritual assignments.

When a cycle repeats, it's a signal that a spiritual pattern is demanding recognition.

Some call it "bad luck" or "just how things go for me." No, beloved — it's a spiritual rhythm that must be interrupted. That's why Jesus came *"to destroy the works of the devil" (1 John 3:8 KJV).*

Destruction begins with recognition. Until you name the pattern, you cannot dismantle it.

Every repeated pain has a root. Every recurring frustration has a spiritual origin. The familiar spirit binds you to what you survived so you never step into what you're called to.

When Comfort Becomes Captivity

Many believers unknowingly confuse peace with comfort. Peace is spiritual alignment; comfort is emotional convenience. God will often disturb your comfort to deliver your destiny.

When Jonah fled from his assignment, he found a ship that matched his disobedience — the Bible says he *"paid the fare" (Jonah 1:3 ESV)*. There is always a cost to choosing the familiar.

God will not allow you to be at peace with what He's trying to deliver you from. That uneasy stirring you feel is divine discomfort. It's the Holy Spirit saying, "You've been here long enough."

Breaking the Emotional Covenant with the Old You

Deliverance is not only about casting out demons; it is about renouncing agreements with your old identity.

Your past self-had habits, responses, and mindsets that no longer belong to you. But the familiar spirit convinces you that the "old you" is still needed for survival.

That's why Paul wrote, *"Put off your old self, which belongs to your former manner of life... and be renewed in the spirit of your mind"* Ephesians 4:22–23 ESV.

You cannot walk in newness while secretly protecting the old. You cannot decree freedom while defending dysfunction. You must divorce the version of you that pain created. The old self is a counterfeit comforter — it kept you alive during trauma, but it cannot lead you into transformation.

The Prophetic Call to Turn Northward

When God said in Deuteronomy 2:3 AMP, "You have circled this mountain long enough," it was a command to shift direction.

Mountains represent cycles. Circling represents delay. North represents destiny.

God is saying, "Stop rehearsing what I've already delivered you from."

Turning northward means elevation — moving higher, even if it costs comfort. It means trusting that the unknown with God is safer than the familiar without Him.

The enemy doesn't need to re-enslave you if he can simply keep you circling.

But today, the Spirit of the Lord declares: **The circle is broken.**

Apostolic Insight

Deliverance demands relocation — mental, emotional, and spiritual. If you do not move, your miracle cannot manifest. Heaven has already released your freedom; now you must walk it out by leaving the atmosphere where your bondage was born.

Your future does not speak the language of your past. Refuse to answer when the old you calls. Refuse to entertain the familiar. The price of newness is separation — but the reward is transformation.

You have circled long enough. It's time to turn northward.

Notes for Freedom Walking

_____

_____

_____

_____

_____

_____

The Familiar Spirit of the Old Self

CHAPTER 4
Forgiveness — The Gate of Release

"And when you stand praying, forgive, if you have anything against anyone; so that your Father also who is in heaven may forgive you your trespasses." **Mark 11:25 ESV**

Forgiveness is the gate through which deliverance becomes freedom. You can cast out spirits, renounce lies, and break covenants, but until forgiveness flows, the door of your soul remains partially shut.

Unforgiveness is the invisible chain that keeps yesterday's pain anchored in today's emotions. It is the rope that ties the wound to the memory, forcing you to relive what you should have released.

The enemy does not mind your prayer life if he can keep you bitter. He does not fear your worship if he can keep you offended. Bitterness is the corrosion of spiritual authority — it eats away at discernment, dulls compassion, and distorts perspective.

Forgiveness is not for the offender; it's for the freed. It is Heaven's strategy to release you from the emotional jurisdiction of your past.

The Misunderstanding of Forgiveness

Forgiveness has been misrepresented as weakness — as if letting go means letting them win. But in the Kingdom, forgiveness is warfare. It is how you close demonic doors that were opened through betrayal, rejection, or injustice.

When Jesus said, *"Father, forgive them; for they know not what they do" (Luke 23:34 ESV),* He wasn't excusing sin — He was revealing spiritual victory. His forgiveness disarmed hell's claim on humanity.

Forgiveness is not denial. It does not erase memory; it redeems it. It does not mean trust must be instantly restored, but it does mean the poison of offense must be removed from your system.

Unforgiveness: The Hidden Gatekeeper

Unforgiveness acts like a spiritual gatekeeper — it guards pain and keeps healing out. Every time you replay what was done, your emotions become a courtroom where the offender is retried daily and you serve as both judge and prisoner.

This is why *Hebrews 12:15 ESV* warns us, *"See to it that no "root of bitterness" springs up and causes trouble, and by it many become defiled."*

Bitterness contaminates destiny. It doesn't just

affect you; it infects everything connected to you; your relationships, ministry, and perception. You can prophesy accurately but love poorly when bitterness rules the heart.

Forgiveness reclaims your authority to love without condition, to lead without contamination, and to see without distortion.

Forgiveness as a Weapon

Forgiveness is not passive; it is an offensive weapon. It dismantles the legal rights of the enemy. When you forgive, you sever his grounds for accusation.

Revelation 12:10 ESV calls him *"the accuser of the brethren."* He cannot accuse what Heaven has already absolved. That's why forgiveness is often the final step in deliverance.

When you forgive, you silence the voice that keeps rehearsing the wound. You declare that vengeance belongs to God *(Romans 12:19 ESV)*, and you remove yourself from the battlefield of the flesh.

Forgiveness says: "I trust God to judge rightly and heal completely." When you release others, you release yourself. When you unclench your fists from the offense, your hands become free to receive restoration.

The Weight of the Unforgiven

Some believers carry people they've never forgiven like invisible weights. You may not see them, but you feel them — in your exhaustion, in your hesitation, in your lack of joy.

Unforgiveness makes the soul heavy because it anchors you to an emotional graveyard. That is why Jesus said in *Matthew 18:21–22 KJV* that forgiveness must be continuous — *"seventy times seven."* Not because the offender deserves it, but because your peace requires it. Forgiveness is maintenance for the soul. It keeps your spiritual oxygen flowing freely.

Forgiving Yourself

Perhaps the hardest forgiveness is inward. You've repented, you've prayed, you've wept — but guilt still whispers, "You should have known better."

Beloved, hear this: forgiveness must flow in every direction — toward others, toward yourself, and toward God for what you misunderstood in the moment.

Psalm 103:12 ESV declares, *"As far as the east is from the west, so far has He removed our transgressions from us."*

If God has released it, who are you to hold it? The Cross is not partial redemption; it is total remission. You must forgive yourself so that grace can complete its work in you.

Apostolic Insight

Forgiveness unlocks realms of divine justice. When you forgive, Heaven moves on your behalf. Forgiveness shifts judgment from your hands into God's — and when Heaven vindicates, restoration follows.

Do not let your heart become a holding cell for those who hurt you. You were never called to carry their sentence — only your assignment. Lay it down, release it, and watch the floodgates of grace open.

Forgiveness is not the end of your deliverance — it is the doorway into restoration. And once you walk through that gate, the sound of your chains will become the sound of your testimony.

Notes for Freedom Walking

_____

_____

_____

_____

_____

Forgiveness — The Gate Of Release

CHAPTER 5
The Power of Confrontation

"And you shall know the truth, and the truth shall make you free." **John 8:32 NKJV**

Deliverance begins where denial ends. There can be no transformation until there is confrontation — not with demons first, but with truth. Truth is Heaven's scalpel. It does not wound to destroy; it cuts to heal.

Confrontation is not cruelty; it is clarity. It is the moment you stop calling your bondage a burden and start naming it for what it is — an intruder in the territory of your destiny.

Every true move of God begins with confrontation. Before there was a resurrection, there was a cross. Before there was a crown, there was a Garden called Gethsemane. Deliverance cannot occur where truth is not welcome.

The Courage to See What You've Avoided

Many avoid confrontation because it demands exposure. We fear seeing ourselves beyond the mask of ministry or the rhythm of routine. But wholeness cannot heal what you hide. God cannot deliver what you still defend.

When Jesus met the man at the pool of Bethesda, He asked, *"Do you want to be made whole?"* *(John 5:6 KJV).*

That question was not rhetorical — it was revelatory. Jesus was confronting the man's mindset before healing his body. Because sometimes, people love the attention of affliction more than the discipline of deliverance.

To confront truth means to face your part in the pain — your agreements, your silence, your avoidance. You may not have started it, but you've learned to live with it. Yet the Holy Spirit is saying: "It's time to stop adjusting to dysfunction."

Truth as a Deliverer

Jesus didn't say, "You shall feel the truth." He said, "You shall know the truth." Truth doesn't cater to emotion; it commands alignment.

When light exposes darkness, there's no debate — the darkness must flee *(John 1:5 ESV).* Confrontation is Heaven's light switch. When you turn it on, what's been hiding loses power. Truth is deliverance without theatrics. It is the quiet authority that dethrones lies. The enemy's greatest weapon is deception, and your greatest weapon is revelation. Every lie you uncover becomes territory you reclaim.

The Pain of Exposure

Exposure is uncomfortable because it dismantles illusion. When God shines a light on hidden motives or secret pain, it is not to shame you — it is to free you. Shame binds, but truth restores.

Adam hid among the trees because sin birthed shame, but God still called his name *(Genesis 3:9 TPT)*. That call was not accusation; it was invitation. Even after exposure, grace was waiting.

Confrontation is love in its most honest form. God loves you too much to let you live comfortably in chains. He will interrupt your peace to secure your purity.

Confronting the Demons Within

Some battles are not external — they are internal negotiations. The unspoken compromises, the hidden grudges, the quiet fears — these are the "demons" that sit unchallenged because they wear the face of reason.

When Jesus faced Legion, He demanded identification: *"What is your name?" (Mark 5:9 ESV)*. Naming the spirit stripped it of anonymity. The same principle holds true for you: what you refuse to name, you give permission to remain.

Confrontation doesn't always look like shouting — sometimes it's a whisper of decision: "No more."

"This pattern stops with me."
"This wound will not define me another day."

That's deliverance in motion — when truth finally meets decision.

Prophetic Confrontation and Apostolic Order

In apostolic deliverance, confrontation restores divine order. You cannot establish Kingdom order where truth is absent. Prophets expose; apostles establish. One reveals the disorder, the other rebuilds the structure.

That's why Paul confronted Peter to his face *(Galatians 2:11 TPT)*. It wasn't malice — it was maintenance. The purity of the Gospel was at stake. Likewise, confrontation in your life is not condemnation; it's construction. God is rebuilding what compromise tried to collapse.

Confrontation is the proof that you value your future more than your feelings.

Confrontation with Love

Truth without love is brutality; love without truth is compromise. The power of confrontation lies in the balance of both. *Ephesians 4:15 ESV* commands us to *"speak the truth in love."* Love ensures that confrontation heals instead of humiliates.

God will often send someone to confront you not to condemn you, but to confirm your calling by removing the residue that's dulling your shine. When truth confronts with love, correction becomes invitation — not rejection.

Apostolic Insight

Deliverance is confrontation. You cannot counsel what you must cast out, and you cannot cast out what you refuse to confront. Confrontation is not conflict; it is clarity. It is Heaven's announcement that the cycle is over.

Beloved, the greatest victory of your life will not come from avoiding battles but from facing them in truth. Do not fear confrontation — it is the key that unlocks transformation. What you expose to the light loses its license to operate in darkness. Confrontation is your weapon. Use it boldly. Use it wisely. Use it with love. For when truth stands tall, freedom cannot be denied.

Notes for Freedom Walking

_____

_____

_____

_____

_____

_____

The Power of Confrontation

CHAPTER 6
Healing the Fractured Soul

"He restoreth my soul: He leadeth me in the paths of righteousness for His name's sake."
Psalm 23:3 KJV

Deliverance is not complete until the soul is healed. The casting out of spirits is the beginning; the restoration of the soul is the completion. Many walk away from the altar free in spirit but still fractured in soul — pieces of themselves scattered across years of pain, betrayal, or loss. But beloved, the God who delivers you is the same God who gathers you. He does not just break chains — He binds up the broken.

The psalmist said, "He restoreth my soul." Restoration means something was once whole, then broken, and now rebuilt. Your soul — your mind, will, and emotions — was designed to function in divine harmony. Trauma disrupts that harmony, creating fragments that respond separately instead of as one. Healing is the holy work of bringing you back into yourself under the Lordship of Christ.

Understanding the Fractured Soul

When trauma occurs, the soul often fragments as a survival mechanism. You learn to function while hiding pain in compartments — the strong side, the spiritual side, the silent side. You become many versions of yourself, switching identities depending on the environment.

You can lead powerfully and still cry privately. You can minister to others and still feel emotionally numb. This is not hypocrisy — it is fragmentation. The Lord understands the secret exhaustion of the divided self.

That's why *Psalm 34:18 ESV* says, *"The Lord is near to the brokenhearted and saves the crushed in spirit."* God comes close to the shattered because only His presence can make the scattered whole again.

The Ministry of the Holy Spirit: The Divine Counselor

Healing the soul is not the work of willpower — it is the ministry of the Holy Spirit. Jesus called Him *"the Comforter" (John 14:26 KJV),* but that word also means Advocate, Counselor, Restorer.

The Holy Spirit does not just soothe pain; He interprets it. He reveals the root of wounds that the mind has buried and the heart has mislabeled.

There are times in prayer when the Spirit will bring to memory something you thought you forgot. That is not regression — it is redemption. He brings it back so He can heal it in His light. Healing requires remembering, but through revelation, not reliving.

You cannot heal what you refuse to feel, and you cannot feel what you continually suppress. The Spirit gives you courage to confront pain without being consumed by it.

The Layers of Healing

Healing comes in layers, just as wounding came in layers. Some wounds are surface — healed by confession and forgiveness. Others are deep — healed by revelation and time in His presence.

David said, *"Search me, O God, and know my heart; try me, and see if there be any wicked way in me" (Psalm 139:23–24 KJV).* That was not a prayer of guilt; it was a prayer of permission. David gave God access to hidden chambers of his soul.

Every layer that God exposes, He intends to heal. Every tear is an invitation. Every trembling moment in prayer is a transaction — pain exchanged for peace, fear traded for faith, shame replaced with glory.

Soul Wounds and Spiritual Identity

When the soul is fractured, identity becomes blurred. You begin to measure yourself by your wounds instead of your worth. You say things like, "I'm just not good enough," or "I guess this is my cross to bear." But beloved, you are not your trauma — you are His testimony.

Isaiah 61:7 KJV declares, *"For your shame ye shall have double."* That means every place where the soul has been wounded, God intends to multiply restoration. The enemy loves fractured people because fractured people cannot stand in full authority.

That's why Jesus told Peter, *"When you are converted, strengthen your brethren" (Luke 22:32 KJV).* Conversion there means restored to wholeness. Peter's denial had split him with guilt, but Christ's love stitched him back together through forgiveness and recommissioning. Wholeness became his new weapon.

Integration: When the Pieces Come Home

The end goal of soul healing is integration — when all the fragments of who you are finally submit to one voice, one purpose, one peace. When the "you" that worships, the "you" that remembers, and the "you" that survived all come into divine alignment.

The Father says, "Welcome home, My child — not just your spirit, but your soul too." In that moment, clarity returns. You begin to recognize your own reflection without the filter of fear. The sound of confusion quiets. The fog lifts. And you realize — this is what peace feels like when it's whole.

Prophetic Declarations for Restoration

• I am being gathered by God. Every scattered part of me is finding its place in His presence.
• My soul is no longer divided. Every fracture is being sealed by the blood of Jesus.
• I am not who I was when I was wounded. I am who I became through His healing.
• My emotions submit to peace. My mind aligns with truth. My will agrees with Heaven.

Every declaration is a hammer against fragmentation. Each word you speak aligns your soul with divine order.

Apostolic Insight

Wholeness is Heaven's justice for every area hell tried to divide. Deliverance gets you out of bondage, but healing keeps you out. Do not rush the process — restoration is a journey, not a moment. The Holy Spirit is not just visiting you; He is rebuilding you. Every tear that falls is an altar where wholeness is being formed. Every time you surrender, Heaven is stitching something back together.

You are not just delivered — you are being redesigned. The same God who restored David's soul is restoring yours. And when He finishes, you will not only be whole — you will carry the anointing to make others whole.

Notes for Freedom Walking

_____

_____

_____

_____

_____

_____

_____

_____

_____

_____

_____

_____

_____

Walking With the Demons of Your Past

CHAPTER 7
Breaking the "Recycle"

"You have circled this mountain long enough; now turn northward." ***Deuteronomy 2:3 AMP***

There comes a moment in every believer's journey when the Spirit of God repeats a command you've heard before—but this time, with another layer of truth. Earlier in this book, we heard the Lord say, "You have circled this mountain long enough." In that chapter, the Word confronted the familiar pull of the old self. Here, that same command confronts the cycles that attempt to rebuild themselves in your present. This is not about returning to who you were—this is about breaking what keeps trying to return to you.

Deliverance is powerful but maintenance is essential. Too many experience moments of breakthrough but return to the same cycle because they were set free from something, yet never built a structure to stay free in something. Freedom requires stewardship. The anointing breaks yokes, but discipline keeps them broken. If the altar brings you out, the Word must keep you up.

God told Israel, "You have circled this mountain long enough." The mountain represented a pattern — familiar, predictable, and exhausting. Many of God's people love the promise but grow comfortable with the pattern. They keep moving but not advancing. It's time to stop mistaking motion for progress.

The Nature of Cycles

A cycle is a repeated spiritual and emotional pattern that replays until it is confronted by revelation. You think it's just another bad season — but the truth is, it's a spiritual loop.

Same kind of relationship.
Same kind of disappointment.
Same kind of delay.

Cycles feed on denial. They thrive when you say, "This is just how life is for me." But once you identify the pattern, you strip it of its power.

That's why *Hosea 4:6 ESV* says, *"My people are destroyed for lack of knowledge."* The lack isn't always information — it's revelation. When truth enters, cycles collapse.

The Spirit Behind the "Recycle"

There is a spirit that loves to reset what you've overcome. It's not always possession — it's permission. The enemy looks for entry points of exhaustion, disappointment, or disobedience to recycle what you've already been delivered from.

That's why Jesus said, *"When the unclean spirit goes out of a man, it passes through dry places seeking rest... and returns to find the house empty, swept, and garnished"* (Matthew 12:43–45 NKJV).

If you do not fill the space once occupied by bondage with truth, prayer, and structure, that space becomes vulnerable to return. Deliverance without discipleship is an open door. Victory without vigilance is temporary. You must occupy your freedom with spiritual discipline.

The Three Doors of "Recycle"

1. **The Door of Memory:** when nostalgia pulls you back to what hurt you. "It wasn't that bad..." the enemy whispers. But it was bad enough to almost kill you. Don't romanticize Egypt.
2. **The Door of Emotion:** when fatigue makes you vulnerable. Elijah's greatest despair came after his greatest victory *(1 Kings 19)*. Weariness makes you forget your progress.
3. **The Door of Distraction:** when busyness replaces presence. Martha was busy for Jesus, but Mary sat with Jesus *(Luke 10:41–42)*.

Activity without alignment invites recycle.

The Power of Consistency

Breaking cycles requires consistency — not perfection. Every time you worship instead of worry, you are breaking a cycle. Every time you choose forgiveness instead of offense, you are rewriting your story. Every time you speak truth instead of fear, you are closing a demonic loop.

Galatians 6:9 KJV declares, "And let us not be weary in well-doing, for in due season we shall reap, if we faint not."

Cycles end when your consistency becomes louder than your excuses.

Deliverance is the miracle.
Consistency is the method.
Obedience is the maintenance.

When God Interrupts the Loop

Sometimes Heaven will interrupt your cycle through divine disruption — a loss, a delay, a shift. It feels uncomfortable, but it's mercy. God will shut doors that lead you backward. He will remove people who keep you recycled in dysfunction. He will silence voices that remind you of your Egypt.

Deuteronomy 1:6 ESV says, "The Lord our God said to us in Horeb, 'You have stayed long enough at this mountain.'" When God interrupts your loop, it is because He intends to advance your life.

You were not created to repeat deliverance; you were created to reproduce dominion.

Keys to Breaking the "Recycle"

• Renew Your Mind Daily: Transformation is maintained by meditation. *Romans 12:2* reminds us that renewing your mind is not seasonal — it's daily.

• Guard Your Atmosphere: What you listen to, watch, and entertain either strengthens your freedom or feeds your former bondage.

• Walk in Accountability: Freedom flourishes in community. *James 5:16 KJV teaches, "Confess your faults one to another, and pray one for another, that ye may be healed."*

• Stay Aligned with the Word: The Word is your anchor; without it, cycles reset.

The Apostolic Discipline of Freedom

Apostolic grace teaches believers how to sustain what was imparted. It doesn't just celebrate deliverance — it structures it. The early church continued daily in prayer, fellowship, and doctrine *(Acts 2:42 KJV)*. They didn't just have revival — they built rhythm. Freedom is fragile without order.

Deliverance must lead to discipleship, and discipleship must produce dominion. Apostolic deliverance says, "We're not coming back this way again." Once the pattern is revealed, it must be dismantled through daily obedience and spiritual maturity.

Apostolic Insight

Freedom sustained by structure produces legacy. It's not enough to be free for a moment — you must become a house of freedom for generations. When you maintain deliverance, you create a blueprint for others to follow. The true sign of maturity is not how loud you shout, but how long you stay free.

You are not circling this mountain again.
You are ascending.
You are turning northward — higher, deeper, stronger.

The Recycling ends here.

Notes for Freedom Walking

_____

_____

_____

_____

_____

_____

Walking With the Demons of Your Past

CHAPTER 8
Walking in Newness

"Therefore if anyone is in Christ, he is a new creature; old things have passed away; behold, all things have become new."
2 Corinthians 5:17 KJV

Deliverance is not the end of your story — it is the beginning of a new creation. You were not set free simply to testify that you came out, but to demonstrate that you walk differently now. Walking in newness means moving in rhythm with Heaven, no longer reacting to your past but responding to your purpose.

The true evidence of deliverance is not how loudly you shouted when chains fell off, but how quietly you walk in obedience when no one is watching. Freedom is not a feeling — it is a function. It is how you think, speak, and live once the dust of battle settles.

The Birth of the New You

When Christ resurrected, the tomb was empty, but the scars remained. Those scars were not signs of defeat; they were proof of transformation. Likewise, walking in newness does not mean pretending the past never existed — it means your past no longer dictates your future.

Romans 6:4 KJV declares, "Just as Christ was raised from the dead by the glory of the Father, even so we also should walk in newness of life."

That "walk" implies continual progress — a steady pace, one step of obedience after another. The new you must be maintained by new rhythms. You cannot live resurrected while thinking like the buried.

Renewing the Mind for the Journey Ahead

The battlefield of newness is always the mind. Paul instructs, *"And be renewed in the spirit of your mind" (Ephesians 4:23 KJV).*

Renewal is not an event; it is a habit. Every day, you must feed your mind truth until truth becomes your instinct. The old mind operates in reaction — fear, doubt, shame. The renewed mind operates in revelation — faith, peace, and identity.

Each morning, when you declare the Word, you are repainting the canvas of your consciousness. Speak what Heaven says until the old narrative loses sound in your spirit. You are no longer rehearsing pain; you are rehearsing purpose.

Developing New Rhythms

Walking in newness requires new disciplines. **Prayer** must now move from emergency to intimacy. **Worship** must move from routine to relationship. **Study** must move from obligation to revelation.

You are building a new life that can carry the weight of your next assignment. Old cycles break permanently when new patterns are established intentionally. Just as the Israelites built the tabernacle according to divine pattern, you must now structure your life according to divine rhythm.

Morning declarations.
Midday gratitude.
Evening reflection.

These are not rituals — they are reinforcements for your deliverance.

Guarding the Gate of Newness

The enemy cannot destroy what God has restored, but he will attempt to distract it. Guard your gates — your eyes, your ears, your mouth, your relationships.

Proverbs 4:23 KJV says, "Keep your heart with all diligence, for out of it flow the issues of life."

Every gate you guard protects your grace. Every boundary you establish secures your breakthrough.

Newness demands discernment — what you tolerate now can determine what you lose later. Surround yourself with those who speak to your growth, not your grief. Some voices remind you of Egypt; others prepare you for Canaan. Choose wisely, for what you entertain in this season will either cultivate your peace or resurrect your pain.

Becoming a Healer of Others

True freedom always reproduces itself. The same anointing that delivered you now flows through you. You are no longer the wounded — you are the witness. Your testimony becomes a map for those still trapped in cycles.

2 Corinthians 1:4 NKJV declares, "He comforts us in all our tribulation, that we may be able to comfort them which are in any trouble."

Deliverance was never just about you — it was about the generations attached to your yes. When you open your mouth, chains tremble. When you pray, doors unlock. When you walk in love, darkness loses territory.

You are the living proof that redemption works. You are the evidence that resurrection is not just an event — it's a lifestyle.

Living as a Carrier of Presence

Walking in newness is walking in presence. You now live with the awareness that God is not only with you but within you.

Your steps carry His glory.
Your words release His wisdom.
Your compassion reflects His character.

Moses' face shone after encountering God; your life will glow with evidence of His grace. The world does not need another sermon — it needs a demonstration. Your healed life preaches louder than any pulpit.

Apostolic Insight

Those who overcome become deliverers for others. The proof of your transformation is your fruit — the lives changed because you chose wholeness.

Heaven did not deliver you just to shout "I'm free!" — Heaven delivered you to build freedom centers in every space your feet tread.

You are an agent of restoration.
You are an ambassador of healing.
You are Heaven's evidence that broken things can live again.

So, walk — not as the one who escaped, but as the one who now carries keys.

Walk in joy.
Walk in discipline.
Walk in revelation.
Walk in newness.

For the old has passed away. And everything about you — your mind, your story, your sound — has become new.

Notes for Freedom Walking

Walking With the Demons of Your Past

CHAPTER 9
The Journey Continues

"Being confident of this very thing, that He who has begun a good work in you will complete it until the day of Jesus Christ.
"Philippians 1:6 KJV

Deliverance was never meant to be a single encounter; it is a continual unveiling of wholeness. You have not merely survived the process — you have been transformed by it.

The demons of the past no longer define you; they have become the backdrop for your testimony of grace. What once tormented you has now become the territory of your authority. Every tear was a seed. Every wound was a doorway. Every confrontation was a graduation.

You have walked through the shadows, faced the memories, broken the cycles, and learned to stand in truth. Now, you walk as one who knows the Healer, not just the healing.

The journey continues — not backward into pain, but forward into purpose.

The Call to Steward Freedom

Freedom must be nurtured like a garden. You must water it daily with prayer, protect it with worship, and prune it through obedience. You are not called to return to what once held you — you are called to lead others out.

As you go forth, remember: the enemy fears not your shout, but your stability. He trembles when a believer walks in quiet authority, disciplined peace, and unwavering joy. Freedom that lasts is freedom that's stewarded.

The Anointing of the Overcomer

You now carry the mantle of an overcomer. *Revelation 12:11 KJV* declares, *"And they overcame him by the blood of the Lamb and by the word of their testimony."* Your deliverance is not just personal — it is generational. The same power that delivered you now flows through your words, your prayers, your presence.

You are the breaker in your bloodline. You are the evidence of God's promise fulfilled. You are the one who refused to die in the wilderness and chose to cross over into wholeness.

Prophetic Declarations for Continued Freedom

1. I am whole, healed, and walking in divine alignment.
   My spirit, soul, and body are synchronized under Heaven's order.

2. The past no longer speaks for me. Every memory is now a testimony of mercy and grace.

3. I carry the oil of deliverance. Where I go, liberty follows. Where I speak, chains break.

4. Cycles are broken, and new paths are formed.
   My steps are directed by the Spirit; my journey is guided by truth.

5. I walk in peace, authority, and prophetic clarity.
   My freedom will not be forfeited, and my destiny will not be delayed.

Apostolic Charge

Beloved, you have walked through the valley and come out with vision. You have wrestled with shadows and emerged shining with light. Now, stand as a reformer — one who doesn't just celebrate freedom, but creates atmospheres where others can find it.

Let your home become a sanctuary of deliverance. Let your ministry become a center of healing. Let your presence carry the weight of peace that only the delivered can hold.

You are the continuation of the story — the living epistle Paul spoke of. Heaven is writing through your life now, penning new chapters of redemption in every place you walk.

Closing Prayer

Father, in the name of Jesus, thank You for every reader who has journeyed through these pages. Thank You for confronting their pain, healing their wounds, and restoring their souls. I decree that every chain of the past is broken — not temporarily, but eternally. I declare that newness is their portion and wholeness is their reality.

Holy Spirit, breathe upon every heart that has dared to believe again. Fill every empty space with peace, joy, and purpose. Let the oil of deliverance flow from their lives to others. And may they never again walk as victims, but as victors — as those commissioned to bring freedom wherever they go.

In Jesus' name — Amen.

Final Apostolic Insight

Deliverance is not the destination; it is the doorway. From this point forward, every step you take is proof that redemption still works. You have walked with the demons of the past — but now you walk with the authority of the future.

The journey continues... But now, you walk in light, in truth, and in newness of life.

Notes for Freedom Walking

_____

_____

_____

_____

_____

_____

_____

_____

_____

_____

The Journey Continues

Appendix
6 Steps to Self-Deliverance

How to Use This Section Safely, Effectively, and With Confidence

Before you begin the self-deliverance steps that follow, it's important to understand what these steps are, why they matter, and how you should approach them. This process is not a ritual, not a formula, and not a performance. It is a guided, intentional encounter with God—designed to help you close spiritual doors, break unhealthy agreements, and claim freedom that has always been available to you.

Deliverance is not about shouting at darkness; it is about aligning yourself fully with truth so darkness loses its legal right to stay.

Think of this section as a toolbox, not a ceremony. The power doesn't come from the words you speak but from:
• your agreement with God,
• your willingness to release what no longer belongs,
• and your decision to stand in authority.

These steps are meant to be done slowly, reflectively, and prayerfully—not rushed. Pause when something touches your heart or stirs emotion; those moments are indicators that God is highlighting an area for healing.

Who These Steps Are For

These steps are safe and appropriate for anyone who wants to:
• break spiritual oppression or torment,
• close open doors from past pain, sin, trauma, or generational patterns,
• renounce unhealthy beliefs or agreements,
• experience emotional or spiritual freedom,
• reset their identity in Christ and reclaim authority.

You do not need to feel spiritually strong, perfect, or knowledgeable. You only need to be willing.

What You Can Expect

It's normal to experience:
• emotional release (crying, trembling, relief),
• mental clarity or lightness,
• a sense of peace or pressure lifting,
• conviction or sudden realizations.

Some may feel nothing at all in the moment—and that's okay. Deliverance is not measured by sensations but by shifts in alignment and authority.

Important Safety Notes

Deliverance is a spiritual and emotional process. Keep these anchors in mind:

- If you have a history of severe trauma, panic disorders, or dissociation, consider doing these steps with a pastor, counselor, or trusted spiritual mentor.
- If something feels overwhelming, stop, breathe, and return when you feel ready.
- If you sense fear, remember: fear is a sign that freedom is close, not a sign to stop.

You are in control at all times.

How to Prepare Before Starting

For the best experience:

1. Find a quiet space where you won't be interrupted.
2. Have a journal nearby to record what comes up.
3. Take a deep breath and invite the Holy Spirit to guide you.
4. Approach this with honesty, not religious pressure.
5. Expect God to meet you—because He will.

A Final Word Before You Begin

You are not about to "fight for freedom."
You are about to stand in freedom already purchased for you.

These steps will help you:
- identify open doors,
- break agreements that empowered oppression,

- renounce lies,
- receive truth,
- and walk forward with clarity and peace.

Take your time.
Move with intention.
And let God do the heavy lifting.

Preparation Prayer

Holy Spirit, I invite You into this moment.
Bring light to every place in me that needs healing, clarity to every lie that needs to be exposed, and strength to every part of me that feels weak or weary.

Jesus, You are my deliverer.
I choose to trust You with my heart, my thoughts, my memories, and my story.
I open my hands and release every burden I've been carrying—anything You never asked me to hold.

Father, surround me with Your peace.
Let Your presence fill this space and settle my mind.
Give me courage to face what You reveal and grace to let go of what no longer belongs to me.

I declare that I am safe in Your love.
I declare that nothing can separate me from Your freedom.
Lead me step by step, and let Your truth guide me into complete wholeness.

Amen.

6 Steps to Self-Deliverance

1. Invite the Holy spirit
2. Confess sin and forgive others
3. Renouce lies, vows, and occult involvement
4. Command spirits to leave in Jesus' name
5. Receive the Holy Spirit and declare Scripture aloud
6. Establish rhythms of discipleship and accountability

Notes for Freedom Walking

_____
_____
_____
_____
_____
_____
_____
_____
_____
_____
_____
_____
_____

Walking With the Demons of Your Past

6 Steps to Self-Deliverance

ARISE & SOAR MENTORSHIP

w/ Dr. Shirley

•••

Mentoring in the areas of:
- Achievement
- Business
- Discipline
- Execution
- Personal Care
- Self Development
- Vision

SCHEDULE A CONSULT SRBMinistries@yahoo.com

Healing takes more than time. It requires truth, awareness, and spiritual authority.

THIS MASTERCLASS ADDRESSES:

- Confronting unresolved wounds from the past
- Breaking cycles that hinder spiritual growth
- Understanding emotional and spiritual triggers
- Walking in healing without shame or condemnation

AVAILABLE FOR CHURCHES, CONFERENCES, AND SMALL GROUPS.

FOR SCHEDULING & INQUIRIES

✉ SRB@DestinyIntMinistries.org

This work was stewarded under the Concise Publishing House imprint, a curated house committed to bringing purpose-driven manuscripts to publication with clarity, integrity, and care.

Publishing & Production
Book Design & Formatting
ISBN & Distribution Guidance
Author Support

www.ConcisePublishing.us

www.ingramcontent.com/pod-product-compliance
Lightning Source LLC
Chambersburg PA
CBHW051700090426
42736CB00013B/2473